For my friends,
family,
and especially
my nephew Ollie.
I love you all so much.

Paddy

Winston

Ike and Dave

left Ollie's house
for the course one day

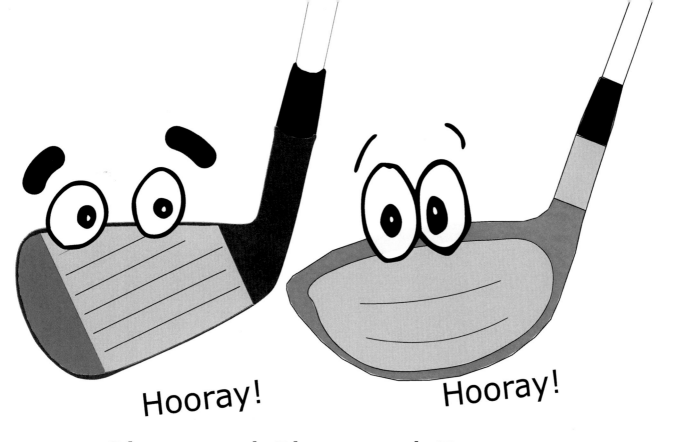

Hooray! Hooray!

Cheered Ike and Dave.
Today's the day we learn to play!

Winston whistled a whimsical tune

while

Paddy proceeded to prod the platoon

Just ye' wait ye' giddy bunch!
Ye' won't be so keen
by the start of lunch.

But why?   But why?

Asked Ike and Dave...

We've heard this game's
so fun to play!

Oh fun ye' say?
Asked Paddy in jest.
Just all ye' wait til ye' face the test!

Just then the trunk popped with
a cheerful clunk

and Ollie their golfer
collected his junk.

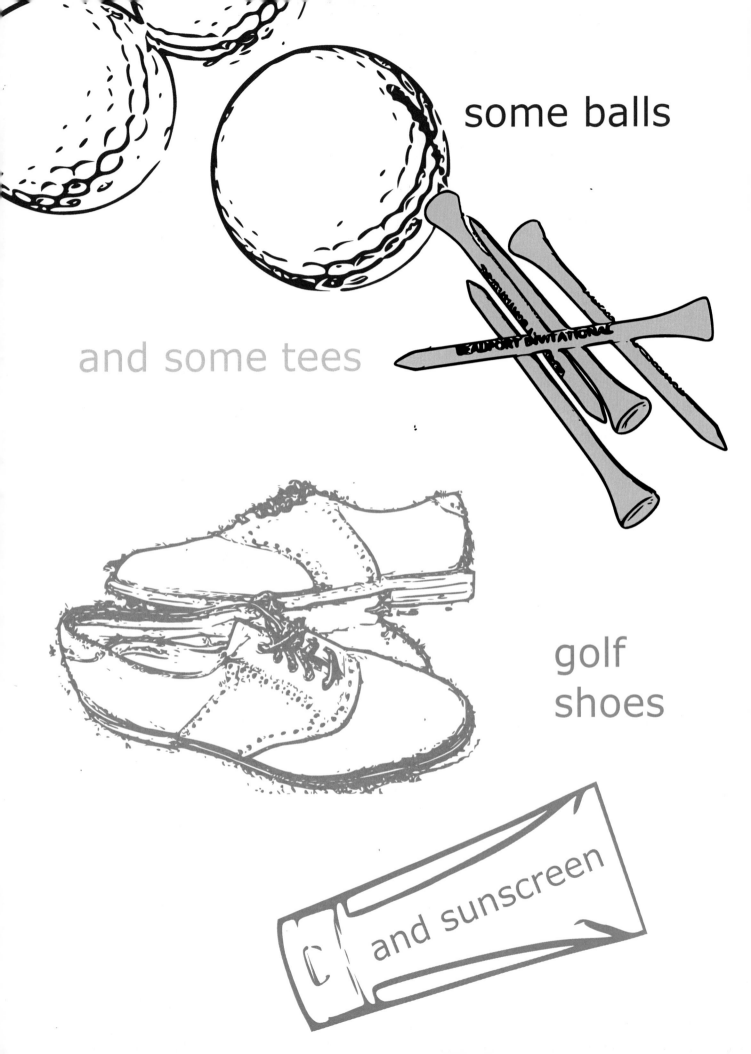

some balls

and some tees

golf
shoes

and sunscreen

Towel rolled by his bag

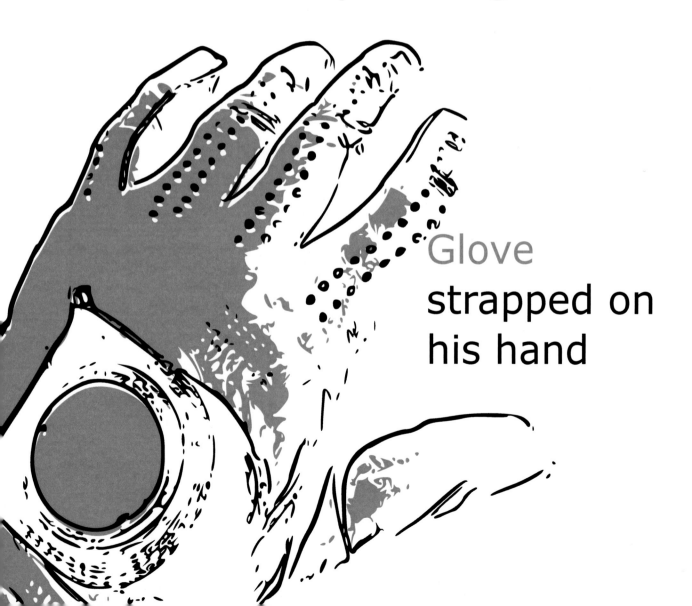

Glove strapped on his hand

Last but not least
to prepare for his round,
Ollie collected the rest of the crowd.

Here's Paddy the Putter
he said at once.
The oldest but wisest
among the bunch.

And Winston oh Winston,

my trusty old wedge,
let's hope for the best
as we re-take the pledge:

To not get too cute
around the greens
and let Paddy take over
in times of need.

Ike and Dave

sat shiny and new,
waiting to learn
of their role in the the crew.

First, Ollie grabbed Ike,
his fancy new iron

and took a few waggles
with his friend Clay admirin'.

A good looking iron,
said Clay about Ike

And man what a driver!
Lemme give it a strike!

You'll get your chance
said Ollie to Clay...

Let's go loosen up.

And they walked to the range.

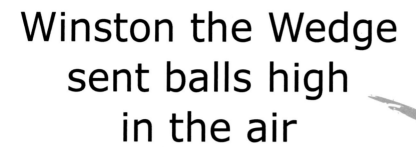

Winston the Wedge
sent balls high
in the air

for short
but tough shots

from sand, grass
and who knows
where!

Ike was up next, and the shots were inspirin'.

Some that curved

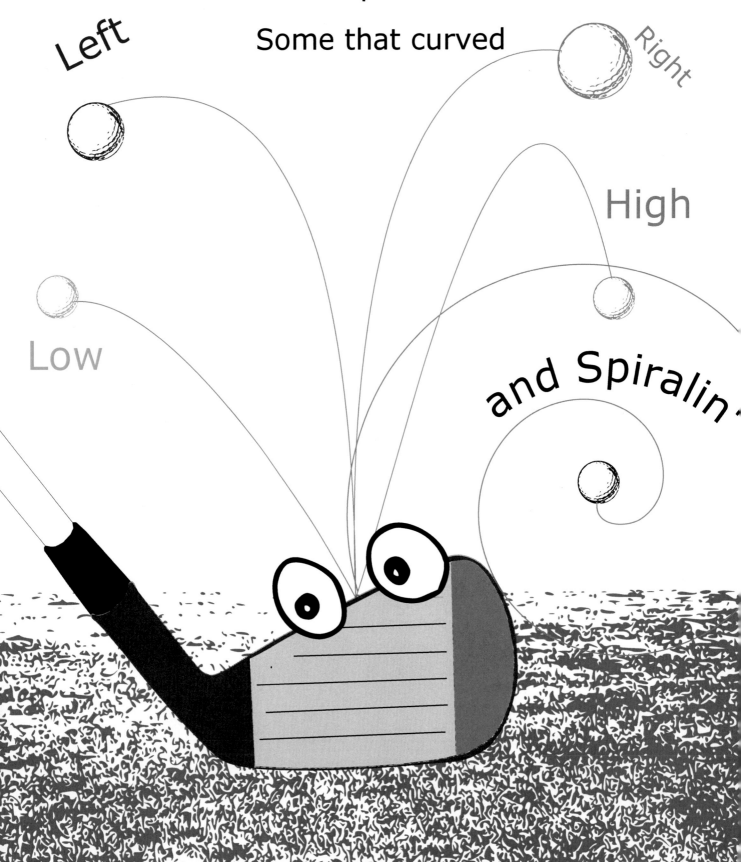

Left

Right

High

Low

and Spiralin'

Then Ollie teed up
a ball for a change

and Dave cranked it
over the net on the range.

Time to go play!
Said Ollie with glee,

And the two happy golfers
walked to the first tee.

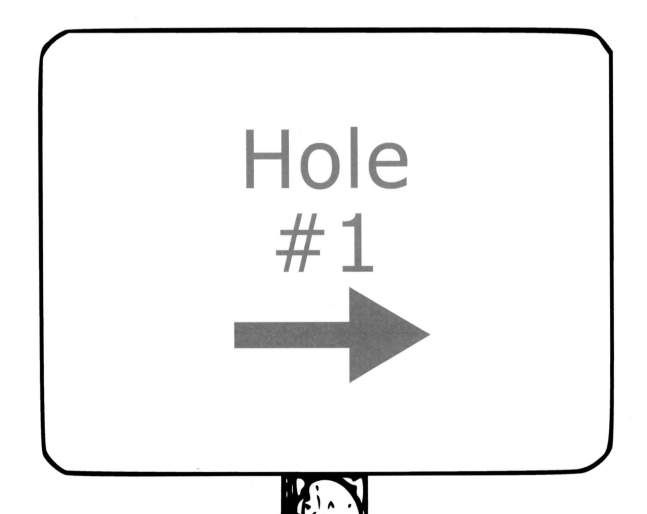

Ollie grabbed Dave,
crushed the ball to its core,
a powerful start
to the opening
par four.

Clay sliced it right
into a small stream
and barely contained
his desire to scream.

Ollie used Ike
to hit for the green
from his most favorite
yardage, one hundred sixteen.

Clay hacked it out of the
boggy ravine,
spraying some mud
on his shirt from the stream.

Now covered in muck, Clay hit for the green, from his least favorite yardage two hundred sixteen.

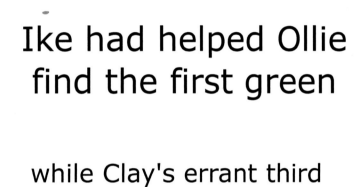

Ike had helped Ollie
find the first green

while Clay's errant third
had traveled
unseen.

I'm done with this hole,
said Clay in a rut
as Ollie lined up his short
birdie putt.

Paddy rolled the ball

in the cup

with great ease,

in one less than par,

we call these

birdies.

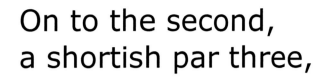

On to the second,
a shortish par three,

where Ollie hit Ike
off a much shorter tee.

The ball started

straight

but the wind
blew it

right

Looking less like a ball
and more like a kite

The ball missed the green
and rolled into the rough
the first chance for

Winston

to show off his stuff.

Clay hit the green,
marked his ball with a spot,
while Ollie prepared
to hit his
flop shot.

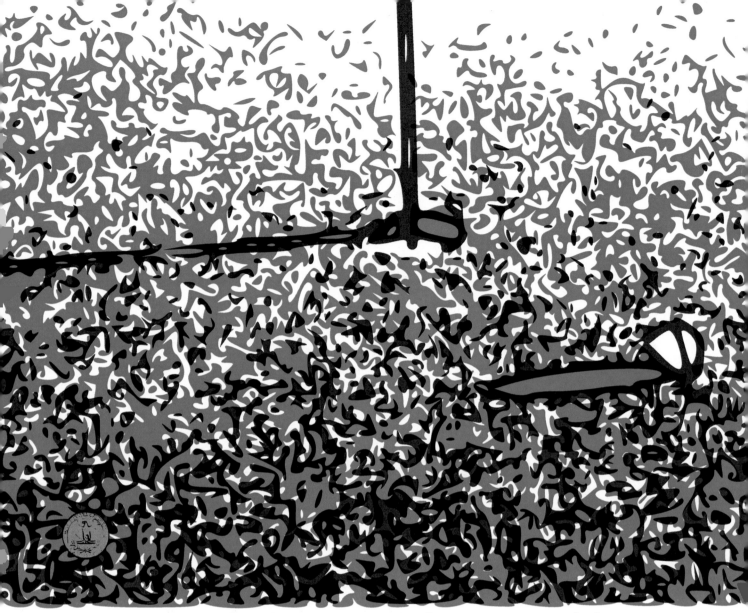

The ball jumped up quickly
with lots of spin

and landed quite gently
right next to the pin.

That's a gimme! Nice par!
said Clay to his friend...

then  his putt

and gave his club
a new

On the third, Ollie drove
where it couldn't
be better,

and Clay hooked it
left
toward the
new shopping center.

While Clay's ball bounced

from parked cars to carts,

Ollie proceeded to throw
in a dart!

A beautiful shot
crushed over a tree,

left Ollie a chance for a
rare eagle three.

Ollie watched proudly as Paddy's
confident roll escorted his ball
to the bottom of the hole.

An eagle! An eagle! How rare is this!?
Cried the once grumpy Paddy
with a new found bliss.

Ollie and Clay continued to play,
having great fun in the warm summer sun.

The twosome made pars on
4,5, and 6

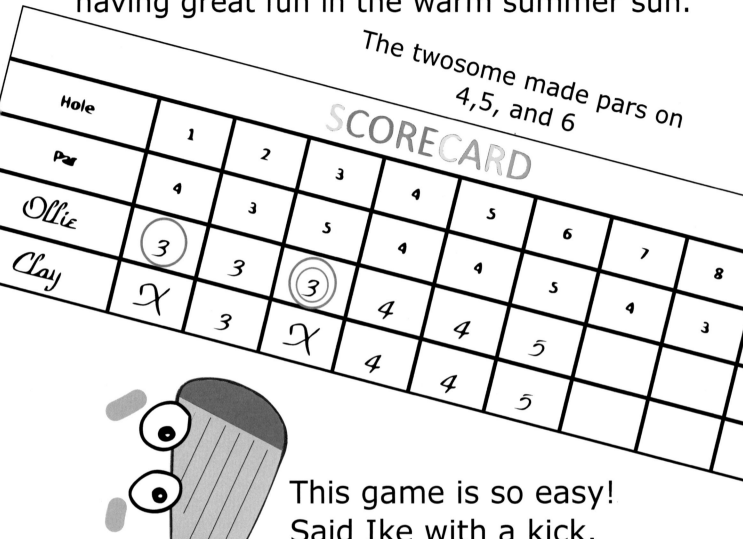

SCORECARD

Hole	1	2	3	4	5	6	7	8
Par	4	3	4	4	5	6	7	8
Ollie	3	3	5	4	4	5	4	3
Clay	X	3	3	4	4	5	4	3

This game is so easy!
Said Ike with a kick.

Not so fast laddy, warned
Paddy to Ike. This round's
not yet over, don't give
up the fight!

Just then on the seventh,
Ike chosen for the shot
proceeded to shank it
clear off of the lot.

I warned ye' teased Paddy
as Ollie dropped a ball

and made triple bogey
once he got his third putt to fall.

SCORECARD

ole	1	2	3	4	5	6	7	8	
Par	4	3	5	4	4	5	4	3	
Ollie	③	3	③	4	4	5	7		
Clau	X	3	X	4	4	5	5		

See! This game is tricky!
Said Paddy
to his chums,
one shot at a time,
and good things will come.

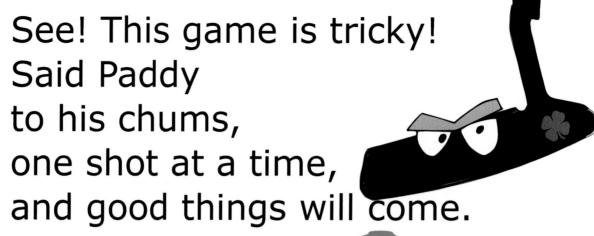

Clay finally
had honors
on the
eighth, a
three par,
but chunked
it so badly
his spine
felt

bizarre.

After filling and smoothing
Clay's divot with sand,
Ollie took Ike into
his right hand

Oh no! Not me!
Cried Ike to his friends.
I can't be trusted
with this task again!

Not to fear laddy!
Said the
kind old Paddy,
that last shot is done!
Focus back on this one.
Score's never the goal,
just fun you see...

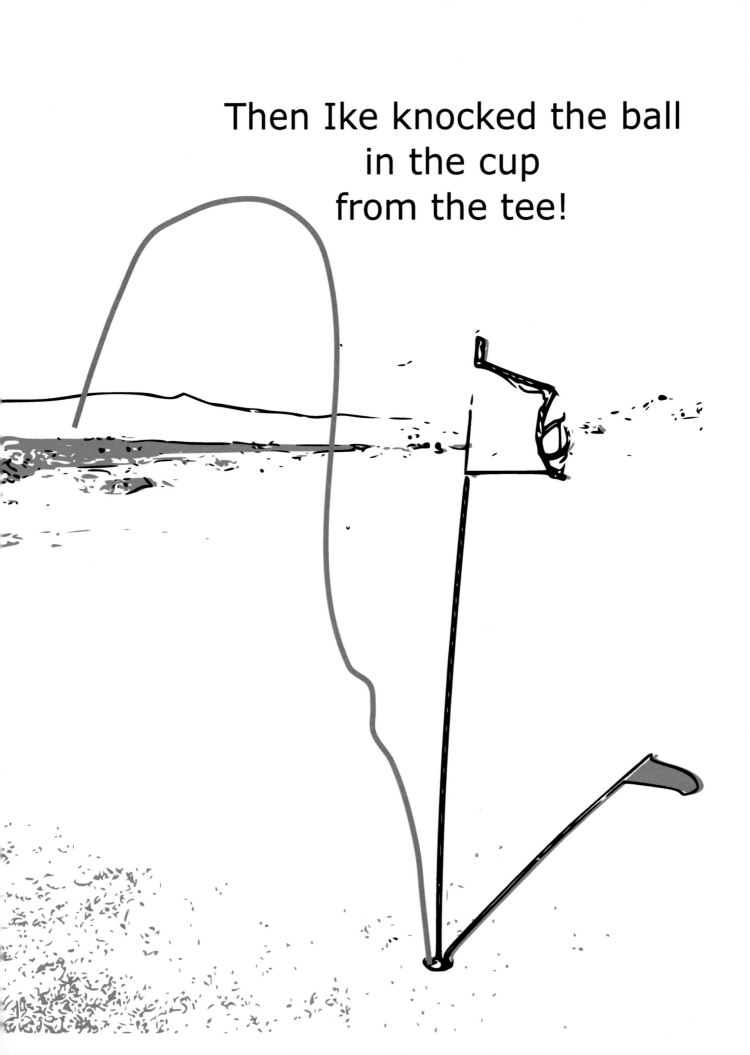

Then Ike knocked the ball
in the cup
from the tee!

My first hole in one!
Yelled an excited Ollie.
One chance in
ten thousand,
the drinks are on me!

Ike couldn't believe
what he had just done.

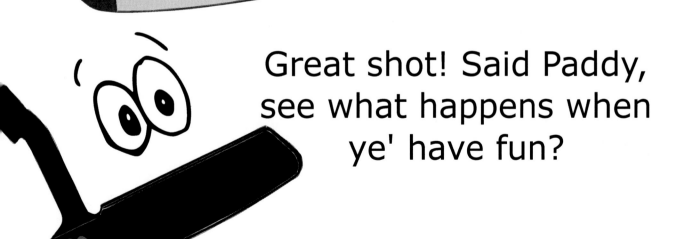

Great shot! Said Paddy,
see what happens when
ye' have fun?

With all the excitement,
Dave blasted a drive
so straight and so far
on hole number nine,

all that was left
from the drive
to the green,
was Ollie's
favorite yardage
one hundred sixteen.

I can make this!
Bragged Ike by mistake,
then hoseled another
into a deep lake.

What happened?
Asked Ike
as he watched
in despair.

One shot at a time
reminded Paddy
with a glare

Don't worry!
Said Winston
as Ollie
dropped a ball.
This game's
about fun!
You can't
control them all.

Trusty old Winston
wedged the ball
on the green,

and Paddy holed
the putt
to help out
the team.

What did I shoot?
Asked Ollie
to his friend.
I lost track
of score
there at the end...

I don't quite know,
said Clay,
let me think....

Well one thing's for sure...

You still owe me
a drink!

33165276R00029

Made in the USA
Columbia, SC
08 November 2018